50 Soups for Every Season Recipes

By: Kelly Johnson

Table of Contents

- Hearty Winter Vegetable Soup
- Spring Pea and Mint Soup
- Chilled Cucumber Soup for Summer
- Autumn Butternut Squash Soup
- Classic Tomato Basil Soup
- French Onion Soup
- Spicy Sweet Potato Soup
- Creamy Broccoli Cheddar Soup
- Spring Leek and Potato Soup
- Roasted Carrot and Ginger Soup
- Warm Lentil Soup with Sausage
- Summer Gazpacho
- Fall Pumpkin Soup
- Chicken Tortilla Soup
- Creamy Mushroom Soup
- Rustic Italian Minestrone
- Chicken and Rice Soup
- Lobster Bisque
- Thai Coconut Curry Soup
- Roasted Cauliflower Soup
- Beet and Apple Soup
- Smoked Salmon Chowder
- Sweet Corn and Shrimp Soup
- Winter Split Pea Soup
- Chunky Beef and Barley Soup
- Creamy Spinach Soup
- New England Clam Chowder
- Spicy Black Bean Soup
- Roasted Garlic and Tomato Soup
- Egg Drop Soup
- Zucchini and Basil Soup
- French-inspired Pot-au-Feu
- Moroccan Chickpea Soup
- Shrimp and Grits Soup
- Curried Carrot and Coconut Soup

- Classic Minestrone with Pesto
- Cold Avocado Soup with Lime
- Curried Squash Soup
- Chicken and Dumplings Soup
- Spinach and White Bean Soup
- Sweet Potato and Black Bean Soup
- Hot and Sour Soup
- Smoked Chicken and Corn Chowder
- Roasted Red Pepper Soup
- Creamy Tomato and Roasted Pepper Soup
- Mushroom and Barley Soup
- Chilled Watermelon Soup
- Gingered Pear and Butternut Soup
- Baked Potato Soup
- Hearty Kale and Sausage Soup

Hearty Winter Vegetable Soup

Ingredients:

- 1 tablespoon olive oil
- 1 onion, chopped
- 2 carrots, peeled and chopped
- 2 celery stalks, chopped
- 2 potatoes, peeled and cubed
- 1 zucchini, chopped
- 1 cup green beans, chopped
- 1 can (14.5 oz) diced tomatoes
- 6 cups vegetable broth
- 2 teaspoons dried thyme
- 1 bay leaf
- Salt and pepper to taste
- 2 cups spinach or kale, chopped

Instructions:

1. In a large pot, heat olive oil over medium heat. Add the onion, carrots, and celery. Sauté for 5 minutes until softened.
2. Add the potatoes, zucchini, green beans, diced tomatoes, vegetable broth, thyme, bay leaf, salt, and pepper.
3. Bring to a boil, then reduce heat and simmer for 30 minutes, until vegetables are tender.
4. Stir in the spinach or kale and cook for another 5 minutes.
5. Remove the bay leaf and serve warm.

Spring Pea and Mint Soup

Ingredients:

- 1 tablespoon olive oil
- 1 onion, chopped
- 4 cups fresh or frozen peas
- 4 cups vegetable broth
- 1/4 cup fresh mint leaves, chopped
- Salt and pepper to taste
- 1/2 cup heavy cream (optional)

Instructions:

1. Heat olive oil in a large pot over medium heat. Add the onion and sauté for 5 minutes until softened.
2. Add the peas and vegetable broth. Bring to a boil, then reduce the heat and simmer for 10 minutes.
3. Stir in the chopped mint leaves and season with salt and pepper.
4. Use an immersion blender to blend the soup until smooth, or transfer to a blender in batches.
5. If desired, stir in heavy cream for a richer texture.
6. Serve garnished with additional mint leaves.

Chilled Cucumber Soup for Summer

Ingredients:

- 2 large cucumbers, peeled and chopped
- 1/2 cup plain yogurt
- 1/4 cup sour cream
- 1 tablespoon olive oil
- 1 tablespoon fresh dill, chopped
- 1 tablespoon lemon juice
- 1 garlic clove, minced
- Salt and pepper to taste

Instructions:

1. Place the cucumbers, yogurt, sour cream, olive oil, dill, lemon juice, garlic, salt, and pepper in a blender.
2. Blend until smooth and creamy.
3. Chill the soup in the refrigerator for at least 2 hours before serving.
4. Serve chilled with additional fresh dill as garnish.

Autumn Butternut Squash Soup

Ingredients:

- 1 medium butternut squash, peeled, seeded, and cubed
- 1 onion, chopped
- 2 carrots, chopped
- 2 tablespoons olive oil
- 4 cups vegetable broth
- 1 teaspoon ground cinnamon
- 1/2 teaspoon ground nutmeg
- Salt and pepper to taste
- 1/2 cup heavy cream (optional)

Instructions:

1. Preheat your oven to 400°F (200°C). Toss the butternut squash, carrots, and onion with olive oil, salt, and pepper. Roast for 25-30 minutes until tender.
2. Transfer the roasted vegetables to a large pot and add the vegetable broth, cinnamon, and nutmeg.
3. Bring to a boil, then reduce to a simmer for 10 minutes.
4. Use an immersion blender to puree the soup until smooth. Alternatively, transfer to a blender.
5. Stir in heavy cream for a richer texture, if desired.
6. Serve hot.

Classic Tomato Basil Soup

Ingredients:

- 2 tablespoons olive oil
- 1 onion, chopped
- 4 garlic cloves, minced
- 4 cups crushed tomatoes (fresh or canned)
- 2 cups vegetable broth
- 1 teaspoon sugar
- Salt and pepper to taste
- 1/2 cup fresh basil leaves, chopped
- 1/2 cup heavy cream (optional)

Instructions:

1. Heat olive oil in a large pot over medium heat. Add the onion and garlic, and sauté for 5 minutes until softened.
2. Add the crushed tomatoes, vegetable broth, sugar, salt, and pepper. Bring to a boil, then reduce the heat and simmer for 20 minutes.
3. Stir in the fresh basil and cook for another 5 minutes.
4. Use an immersion blender to puree the soup until smooth, or transfer to a blender.
5. For a creamier texture, stir in heavy cream before serving.
6. Serve with fresh basil leaves for garnish.

French Onion Soup

Ingredients:

- 4 large onions, thinly sliced
- 2 tablespoons butter
- 1 tablespoon olive oil
- 4 cups beef broth
- 1 cup white wine
- 1 tablespoon fresh thyme, chopped
- 1 tablespoon flour
- Salt and pepper to taste
- 4 slices baguette
- 1 cup Gruyère cheese, grated

Instructions:

1. In a large pot, heat butter and olive oil over medium heat. Add the onions and cook, stirring occasionally, for 30-40 minutes, until deeply caramelized.
2. Add the flour and cook for 2 minutes. Then add the white wine, scraping up any bits from the bottom of the pot.
3. Add the beef broth, thyme, salt, and pepper. Bring to a boil, then reduce to a simmer and cook for 15 minutes.
4. Preheat your broiler. Ladle the soup into oven-safe bowls and top each with a slice of baguette and grated Gruyère cheese.
5. Broil for 3-5 minutes, until the cheese is melted and golden.
6. Serve hot.

Spicy Sweet Potato Soup

Ingredients:

- 2 medium sweet potatoes, peeled and cubed
- 1 onion, chopped
- 2 tablespoons olive oil
- 1 teaspoon ground cumin
- 1 teaspoon chili powder
- 4 cups vegetable broth
- Salt and pepper to taste
- 1/2 cup coconut milk (optional)

Instructions:

1. Heat olive oil in a large pot over medium heat. Add the onion and sauté for 5 minutes until softened.
2. Add the sweet potatoes, cumin, chili powder, vegetable broth, salt, and pepper. Bring to a boil, then reduce heat and simmer for 20 minutes until the sweet potatoes are tender.
3. Use an immersion blender to puree the soup until smooth, or transfer to a blender.
4. Stir in coconut milk for a creamy texture, if desired.
5. Serve hot.

Creamy Broccoli Cheddar Soup

Ingredients:

- 1 tablespoon butter
- 1 onion, chopped
- 2 garlic cloves, minced
- 4 cups broccoli florets
- 4 cups vegetable broth
- 1 cup heavy cream
- 2 cups sharp cheddar cheese, shredded
- Salt and pepper to taste

Instructions:

1. Melt butter in a large pot over medium heat. Add the onion and garlic, and sauté for 5 minutes until softened.
2. Add the broccoli and vegetable broth, and bring to a boil. Reduce the heat and simmer for 10 minutes, until the broccoli is tender.
3. Use an immersion blender to puree the soup until smooth, or transfer to a blender.
4. Stir in heavy cream and shredded cheddar cheese until the cheese melts and the soup becomes creamy.
5. Season with salt and pepper, and serve hot.

Spring Leek and Potato Soup

Ingredients:

- 2 tablespoons butter
- 2 leeks, cleaned and sliced
- 2 potatoes, peeled and cubed
- 4 cups vegetable broth
- 1/2 cup heavy cream (optional)
- Salt and pepper to taste

Instructions:

1. In a large pot, melt butter over medium heat. Add the leeks and sauté for 5 minutes until softened.
2. Add the potatoes and vegetable broth. Bring to a boil, then reduce the heat and simmer for 20 minutes, until the potatoes are tender.
3. Use an immersion blender to puree the soup until smooth, or transfer to a blender.
4. Stir in heavy cream for a richer texture, if desired.
5. Season with salt and pepper, and serve hot.

Roasted Carrot and Ginger Soup

Ingredients:

- 1 lb carrots, peeled and chopped
- 1 tablespoon olive oil
- 1 onion, chopped
- 2 teaspoons fresh ginger, grated
- 4 cups vegetable broth
- Salt and pepper to taste
- 1/4 cup coconut milk (optional)

Instructions:

1. Preheat the oven to 400°F (200°C). Toss the carrots with olive oil, salt, and pepper. Roast for 20-25 minutes until tender.
2. In a large pot, sauté the onion and ginger for 5 minutes.
3. Add the roasted carrots and vegetable broth, and bring to a boil. Reduce the heat and simmer for 10 minutes.
4. Use an immersion blender to puree the soup until smooth, or transfer to a blender.
5. Stir in coconut milk for a creamy texture, if desired.
6. Serve hot.

Warm Lentil Soup with Sausage

Ingredients:

- 1 tablespoon olive oil
- 1 onion, chopped
- 2 garlic cloves, minced
- 2 carrots, peeled and chopped
- 2 celery stalks, chopped
- 1 pound Italian sausage (bulk or casing removed)
- 1 cup dried lentils, rinsed
- 6 cups chicken broth
- 1 bay leaf
- 1 teaspoon dried thyme
- Salt and pepper to taste
- 2 cups spinach or kale, chopped

Instructions:

1. Heat olive oil in a large pot over medium heat. Add the onion, garlic, carrots, and celery, and sauté for 5-7 minutes until softened.
2. Add the sausage to the pot and cook, breaking it up with a spoon, until browned.
3. Add the lentils, chicken broth, bay leaf, thyme, salt, and pepper. Bring to a boil, then reduce the heat and simmer for 30-35 minutes, until the lentils are tender.
4. Stir in the spinach or kale and cook for another 5 minutes.
5. Remove the bay leaf and serve hot.

Summer Gazpacho

Ingredients:

- 4 ripe tomatoes, chopped
- 1 cucumber, peeled and chopped
- 1 bell pepper, chopped
- 1 small red onion, chopped
- 2 garlic cloves, minced
- 2 cups tomato juice
- 1/4 cup olive oil
- 2 tablespoons red wine vinegar
- 1 tablespoon lemon juice
- Salt and pepper to taste
- Fresh basil or parsley for garnish

Instructions:

1. In a blender or food processor, combine the tomatoes, cucumber, bell pepper, onion, garlic, tomato juice, olive oil, red wine vinegar, and lemon juice.
2. Blend until smooth, or leave it slightly chunky if desired.
3. Season with salt and pepper to taste.
4. Chill the gazpacho in the refrigerator for at least 2 hours before serving.
5. Garnish with fresh basil or parsley before serving.

Fall Pumpkin Soup

Ingredients:

- 1 medium pumpkin, peeled, seeded, and cubed (or 1 can pumpkin puree)
- 1 onion, chopped
- 2 tablespoons olive oil
- 3 cups vegetable broth
- 1 teaspoon ground cinnamon
- 1/2 teaspoon ground nutmeg
- 1/4 teaspoon ground ginger
- Salt and pepper to taste
- 1/2 cup heavy cream (optional)

Instructions:

1. In a large pot, heat olive oil over medium heat. Add the onion and sauté for 5 minutes until softened.
2. Add the pumpkin cubes (or pumpkin puree), vegetable broth, cinnamon, nutmeg, ginger, salt, and pepper.
3. Bring to a boil, then reduce the heat and simmer for 20-25 minutes until the pumpkin is tender.
4. Use an immersion blender to puree the soup until smooth, or transfer to a blender.
5. Stir in heavy cream for a richer texture, if desired.
6. Serve hot.

Chicken Tortilla Soup

Ingredients:

- 1 tablespoon olive oil
- 1 onion, chopped
- 2 garlic cloves, minced
- 1 can (14.5 oz) diced tomatoes
- 4 cups chicken broth
- 2 teaspoons chili powder
- 1 teaspoon cumin
- Salt and pepper to taste
- 2 cups cooked chicken, shredded
- 1 cup corn kernels (fresh, frozen, or canned)
- Tortilla strips or chips for garnish
- Fresh cilantro and lime wedges for garnish

Instructions:

1. Heat olive oil in a large pot over medium heat. Add the onion and garlic, and sauté for 5 minutes until softened.
2. Add the diced tomatoes, chicken broth, chili powder, cumin, salt, and pepper. Bring to a boil, then reduce the heat and simmer for 15 minutes.
3. Stir in the shredded chicken and corn. Simmer for an additional 10 minutes.
4. Ladle the soup into bowls and top with tortilla strips or chips, fresh cilantro, and a lime wedge.
5. Serve hot.

Creamy Mushroom Soup

Ingredients:

- 2 tablespoons butter
- 1 onion, chopped
- 3 garlic cloves, minced
- 1 lb mushrooms, sliced (such as cremini, button, or a mix)
- 1 teaspoon fresh thyme, chopped
- 4 cups vegetable broth
- 1 cup heavy cream
- Salt and pepper to taste
- Fresh parsley for garnish

Instructions:

1. Melt butter in a large pot over medium heat. Add the onion and garlic, and sauté for 5 minutes until softened.
2. Add the mushrooms and thyme, and cook for 10 minutes, until the mushrooms release their moisture and become tender.
3. Add the vegetable broth and bring to a boil. Reduce the heat and simmer for 15 minutes.
4. Use an immersion blender to puree the soup until smooth, or transfer to a blender.
5. Stir in the heavy cream, salt, and pepper, and cook for an additional 5 minutes.
6. Garnish with fresh parsley before serving.

Rustic Italian Minestrone

Ingredients:

- 2 tablespoons olive oil
- 1 onion, chopped
- 2 garlic cloves, minced
- 2 carrots, peeled and chopped
- 2 celery stalks, chopped
- 1 zucchini, chopped
- 1 can (14.5 oz) diced tomatoes
- 4 cups vegetable broth
- 1 can (15 oz) cannellini beans, drained and rinsed
- 1/2 cup small pasta (like elbow or ditalini)
- 1 cup spinach or kale, chopped
- Salt and pepper to taste
- Fresh Parmesan cheese for garnish

Instructions:

1. Heat olive oil in a large pot over medium heat. Add the onion, garlic, carrots, and celery, and sauté for 5-7 minutes until softened.
2. Add the zucchini, diced tomatoes, vegetable broth, cannellini beans, pasta, and salt and pepper. Bring to a boil, then reduce the heat and simmer for 20 minutes until the vegetables are tender and the pasta is cooked.
3. Stir in the spinach or kale and cook for another 5 minutes.
4. Serve the soup garnished with fresh Parmesan cheese.

Chicken and Rice Soup

Ingredients:

- 1 tablespoon olive oil
- 1 onion, chopped
- 2 garlic cloves, minced
- 2 carrots, peeled and chopped
- 2 celery stalks, chopped
- 4 cups chicken broth
- 1 cup cooked chicken, shredded
- 1/2 cup rice (white or brown)
- 1 teaspoon dried thyme
- Salt and pepper to taste
- 2 cups spinach or kale, chopped (optional)

Instructions:

1. Heat olive oil in a large pot over medium heat. Add the onion, garlic, carrots, and celery, and sauté for 5 minutes until softened.
2. Add the chicken broth, shredded chicken, rice, thyme, salt, and pepper. Bring to a boil, then reduce the heat and simmer for 20 minutes until the rice is tender.
3. Stir in the spinach or kale (if using) and cook for an additional 5 minutes.
4. Serve hot.

Lobster Bisque

Ingredients:

- 1 tablespoon butter
- 1 onion, chopped
- 2 garlic cloves, minced
- 1/2 cup brandy (optional)
- 2 cups lobster stock or seafood broth
- 1 cup heavy cream
- 1/2 lb cooked lobster meat, chopped
- 2 tablespoons tomato paste
- Salt and pepper to taste
- Fresh parsley for garnish

Instructions:

1. Melt butter in a large pot over medium heat. Add the onion and garlic, and sauté for 5 minutes until softened.
2. Add the brandy (if using) and cook for 2-3 minutes until slightly reduced.
3. Add the lobster stock, heavy cream, lobster meat, tomato paste, salt, and pepper. Bring to a boil, then reduce the heat and simmer for 15 minutes.
4. Use an immersion blender to puree the soup until smooth, or transfer to a blender.
5. Serve garnished with fresh parsley.

Thai Coconut Curry Soup

Ingredients:

- 1 tablespoon olive oil
- 1 onion, chopped
- 2 garlic cloves, minced
- 1 tablespoon fresh ginger, grated
- 1 tablespoon red curry paste
- 4 cups coconut milk
- 2 cups vegetable broth
- 1 cup mushrooms, sliced
- 1 cup carrots, sliced
- 1/2 cup bell pepper, sliced
- Salt and pepper to taste
- Fresh cilantro and lime wedges for garnish

Instructions:

1. Heat olive oil in a large pot over medium heat. Add the onion, garlic, and ginger, and sauté for 5 minutes until softened.
2. Stir in the red curry paste and cook for 1 minute.
3. Add the coconut milk, vegetable broth, mushrooms, carrots, bell pepper, salt, and pepper. Bring to a boil, then reduce the heat and simmer for 15-20 minutes until the vegetables are tender.
4. Serve garnished with fresh cilantro and a lime wedge.

Roasted Cauliflower Soup

Ingredients:

- 1 medium cauliflower, cut into florets
- 1 tablespoon olive oil
- 1 onion, chopped
- 3 garlic cloves, minced
- 4 cups vegetable broth
- 1 teaspoon ground cumin
- Salt and pepper to taste
- 1/2 cup coconut milk (optional)

Instructions:

1. Preheat the oven to 400°F (200°C). Toss the cauliflower florets with olive oil, salt, and pepper. Roast for 25-30 minutes until tender and golden.
2. Heat olive oil in a large pot over medium heat. Add the onion and garlic, and sauté for 5 minutes until softened.
3. Add the roasted cauliflower, vegetable broth, cumin, salt, and pepper. Bring to a boil, then reduce the heat and simmer for 10 minutes.
4. Use an immersion blender to puree the soup until smooth, or transfer to a blender.
5. Stir in coconut milk for a creamy texture, if desired.
6. Serve hot.

Beet and Apple Soup

Ingredients:

- 2 medium beets, peeled and diced
- 1 apple, peeled, cored, and chopped
- 1 onion, chopped
- 2 garlic cloves, minced
- 4 cups vegetable broth
- 1 teaspoon ground ginger
- Salt and pepper to taste
- 1 tablespoon olive oil
- Fresh parsley for garnish

Instructions:

1. Heat olive oil in a large pot over medium heat. Add the onion and garlic, and sauté for 5 minutes until softened.
2. Add the diced beets, chopped apple, vegetable broth, ginger, salt, and pepper. Bring to a boil, then reduce the heat and simmer for 25-30 minutes, until the beets are tender.
3. Use an immersion blender to puree the soup until smooth, or transfer to a blender.
4. Garnish with fresh parsley and serve hot.

Smoked Salmon Chowder

Ingredients:

- 1 tablespoon butter
- 1 onion, chopped
- 2 celery stalks, chopped
- 2 garlic cloves, minced
- 2 potatoes, peeled and diced
- 4 cups chicken or vegetable broth
- 1 cup heavy cream
- 1/2 pound smoked salmon, flaked
- 1 tablespoon fresh dill, chopped
- Salt and pepper to taste

Instructions:

1. Melt butter in a large pot over medium heat. Add the onion, celery, and garlic, and sauté for 5 minutes until softened.
2. Add the diced potatoes, broth, salt, and pepper. Bring to a boil, then reduce the heat and simmer for 15-20 minutes, until the potatoes are tender.
3. Stir in the heavy cream and smoked salmon. Cook for 5 more minutes, until the salmon is heated through.
4. Stir in fresh dill and serve hot.

Sweet Corn and Shrimp Soup

Ingredients:

- 1 tablespoon olive oil
- 1 onion, chopped
- 2 garlic cloves, minced
- 2 cups corn kernels (fresh or frozen)
- 4 cups seafood or vegetable broth
- 1 teaspoon chili powder
- 1/2 teaspoon cumin
- 1/2 pound shrimp, peeled and deveined
- Salt and pepper to taste
- Fresh cilantro for garnish

Instructions:

1. Heat olive oil in a large pot over medium heat. Add the onion and garlic, and sauté for 5 minutes until softened.
2. Add the corn kernels, broth, chili powder, cumin, salt, and pepper. Bring to a boil, then reduce the heat and simmer for 15 minutes.
3. Add the shrimp and cook for 3-5 minutes, until they turn pink and are cooked through.
4. Garnish with fresh cilantro and serve hot.

Winter Split Pea Soup

Ingredients:

- 1 tablespoon olive oil
- 1 onion, chopped
- 2 carrots, peeled and chopped
- 2 celery stalks, chopped
- 2 garlic cloves, minced
- 1 1/2 cups dried split peas, rinsed
- 6 cups vegetable or chicken broth
- 1 teaspoon dried thyme
- Salt and pepper to taste
- 1 bay leaf

Instructions:

1. Heat olive oil in a large pot over medium heat. Add the onion, carrots, celery, and garlic, and sauté for 5 minutes until softened.
2. Add the split peas, broth, thyme, salt, pepper, and bay leaf. Bring to a boil, then reduce the heat and simmer for 45-50 minutes, until the peas are tender.
3. Remove the bay leaf and use an immersion blender to puree the soup for a creamy texture (optional).
4. Serve hot.

Chunky Beef and Barley Soup

Ingredients:

- 1 tablespoon olive oil
- 1 pound beef stew meat, cubed
- 1 onion, chopped
- 2 garlic cloves, minced
- 2 carrots, peeled and chopped
- 2 celery stalks, chopped
- 1/2 cup pearl barley
- 6 cups beef broth
- 1 teaspoon dried thyme
- Salt and pepper to taste
- Fresh parsley for garnish

Instructions:

1. Heat olive oil in a large pot over medium heat. Add the beef cubes and cook for 5-7 minutes until browned on all sides.
2. Add the onion, garlic, carrots, and celery, and sauté for 5 minutes until softened.
3. Stir in the barley, beef broth, thyme, salt, and pepper. Bring to a boil, then reduce the heat and simmer for 45-50 minutes, until the barley is tender.
4. Garnish with fresh parsley and serve hot.

Creamy Spinach Soup

Ingredients:

- 1 tablespoon olive oil
- 1 onion, chopped
- 2 garlic cloves, minced
- 1 potato, peeled and chopped
- 4 cups vegetable broth
- 6 cups fresh spinach
- 1 cup heavy cream
- Salt and pepper to taste
- Fresh nutmeg for garnish (optional)

Instructions:

1. Heat olive oil in a large pot over medium heat. Add the onion and garlic, and sauté for 5 minutes until softened.
2. Add the potato and vegetable broth, and bring to a boil. Reduce the heat and simmer for 15-20 minutes, until the potatoes are tender.
3. Stir in the spinach and cook for 5-7 minutes, until wilted.
4. Use an immersion blender to puree the soup until smooth, or transfer to a blender.
5. Stir in the heavy cream and season with salt and pepper.
6. Garnish with a pinch of fresh nutmeg and serve hot.

New England Clam Chowder

Ingredients:

- 2 tablespoons butter
- 1 onion, chopped
- 2 garlic cloves, minced
- 2 cups diced potatoes
- 4 cups clam juice or seafood broth
- 1/2 cup heavy cream
- 1 pound fresh clams, shucked and chopped (or canned clams)
- 1 teaspoon fresh thyme, chopped
- Salt and pepper to taste
- Fresh parsley for garnish

Instructions:

1. Melt butter in a large pot over medium heat. Add the onion and garlic, and sauté for 5 minutes until softened.
2. Add the diced potatoes and clam juice. Bring to a boil, then reduce the heat and simmer for 15-20 minutes, until the potatoes are tender.
3. Stir in the clams, heavy cream, thyme, salt, and pepper. Cook for an additional 5-7 minutes until heated through.
4. Garnish with fresh parsley and serve hot.

Spicy Black Bean Soup

Ingredients:

- 1 tablespoon olive oil
- 1 onion, chopped
- 2 garlic cloves, minced
- 1 tablespoon ground cumin
- 1 tablespoon chili powder
- 2 cans (15 oz each) black beans, drained and rinsed
- 4 cups vegetable broth
- 1/2 cup salsa
- Salt and pepper to taste
- Fresh cilantro for garnish

Instructions:

1. Heat olive oil in a large pot over medium heat. Add the onion and garlic, and sauté for 5 minutes until softened.
2. Stir in the cumin and chili powder, and cook for 1 minute.
3. Add the black beans, vegetable broth, salsa, salt, and pepper. Bring to a boil, then reduce the heat and simmer for 15 minutes.
4. Use an immersion blender to puree the soup partially (or blend a portion for a thicker consistency).
5. Garnish with fresh cilantro and serve hot.

Roasted Garlic and Tomato Soup

Ingredients:

- 1 head of garlic
- 2 tablespoons olive oil
- 2 cans (14.5 oz each) diced tomatoes
- 2 cups vegetable broth
- 1 onion, chopped
- 1 teaspoon dried basil
- Salt and pepper to taste
- 1/2 cup heavy cream (optional)

Instructions:

1. Preheat the oven to 400°F (200°C). Slice the top off the garlic head and drizzle with olive oil. Wrap in foil and roast for 30-40 minutes, until soft.
2. Heat olive oil in a large pot over medium heat. Add the onion and sauté for 5 minutes until softened.
3. Squeeze the roasted garlic into the pot and stir in the diced tomatoes, vegetable broth, basil, salt, and pepper. Bring to a boil, then reduce the heat and simmer for 15 minutes.
4. Use an immersion blender to puree the soup until smooth, or transfer to a blender.
5. Stir in heavy cream for a creamy texture (optional).
6. Serve hot.

Egg Drop Soup

Ingredients:

- 4 cups chicken broth
- 1 tablespoon soy sauce
- 1 teaspoon sesame oil
- 2 eggs, beaten
- 1 tablespoon cornstarch (optional, for thickening)
- 1/4 teaspoon ground white pepper
- 2 green onions, chopped
- 1/2 teaspoon fresh ginger, grated (optional)

Instructions:

1. Bring chicken broth, soy sauce, sesame oil, and white pepper to a simmer in a pot over medium heat.
2. (Optional) If you prefer a thicker soup, dissolve cornstarch in a little water and add to the broth. Stir to combine.
3. Slowly pour the beaten eggs into the simmering broth while stirring gently with a fork or chopsticks to create thin ribbons.
4. Stir in green onions and ginger (if using), then remove from heat.
5. Serve hot, garnished with extra green onions.

Zucchini and Basil Soup

Ingredients:

- 2 tablespoons olive oil
- 1 onion, chopped
- 2 garlic cloves, minced
- 4 zucchinis, chopped
- 4 cups vegetable broth
- 1/2 cup fresh basil leaves
- Salt and pepper to taste
- 1/2 cup heavy cream (optional, for creaminess)

Instructions:

1. Heat olive oil in a large pot over medium heat. Add the onion and garlic, and sauté for 5 minutes until softened.
2. Add the chopped zucchini and cook for an additional 5 minutes.
3. Pour in the vegetable broth and bring the soup to a boil. Reduce the heat and simmer for 15 minutes, until the zucchini is tender.
4. Add the fresh basil and blend the soup with an immersion blender or transfer to a blender until smooth.
5. Stir in heavy cream if desired, and season with salt and pepper.
6. Serve hot with fresh basil as garnish.

French-inspired Pot-au-Feu

Ingredients:

- 2 pounds beef chuck, cut into chunks
- 2 carrots, peeled and chopped
- 2 leeks, trimmed and sliced
- 1 onion, peeled and quartered
- 3 garlic cloves, smashed
- 4 potatoes, peeled and halved
- 2 bay leaves
- 4 cups beef broth
- Salt and pepper to taste
- Fresh parsley for garnish

Instructions:

1. Place beef, carrots, leeks, onion, garlic, potatoes, bay leaves, and beef broth into a large pot. Bring to a boil.
2. Reduce the heat and simmer for 2-3 hours until the beef is tender and the flavors have melded.
3. Remove the beef and vegetables, and season the broth with salt and pepper.
4. Serve the soup with the beef and vegetables, garnished with fresh parsley.

Moroccan Chickpea Soup

Ingredients:

- 2 tablespoons olive oil
- 1 onion, chopped
- 2 garlic cloves, minced
- 1 teaspoon ground cumin
- 1 teaspoon ground coriander
- 1 teaspoon ground cinnamon
- 1 can (15 oz) chickpeas, drained and rinsed
- 4 cups vegetable broth
- 1 can (14.5 oz) diced tomatoes
- 1/4 cup fresh cilantro, chopped
- Salt and pepper to taste
- Lemon wedges for garnish

Instructions:

1. Heat olive oil in a large pot over medium heat. Add the onion and garlic, and sauté for 5 minutes until softened.
2. Stir in the cumin, coriander, and cinnamon, and cook for 1 minute until fragrant.
3. Add the chickpeas, vegetable broth, and diced tomatoes. Bring to a boil, then reduce the heat and simmer for 20 minutes.
4. Stir in fresh cilantro, and season with salt and pepper.
5. Serve with a squeeze of lemon juice for added freshness.

Shrimp and Grits Soup

Ingredients:

- 1 tablespoon olive oil
- 1/2 pound shrimp, peeled and deveined
- 1 onion, chopped
- 2 garlic cloves, minced
- 1 cup cornmeal (for grits)
- 4 cups seafood or chicken broth
- 1 cup milk
- 1/2 teaspoon smoked paprika
- Salt and pepper to taste
- Fresh parsley for garnish

Instructions:

1. Heat olive oil in a large pot over medium heat. Add the shrimp and cook for 2-3 minutes until pink and cooked through. Remove the shrimp and set aside.
2. In the same pot, add the onion and garlic, and sauté for 5 minutes until softened.
3. Add the cornmeal and slowly pour in the broth, whisking to prevent lumps. Bring to a simmer and cook for 10 minutes, until thickened.
4. Stir in the milk, smoked paprika, and season with salt and pepper. Return the shrimp to the pot.
5. Serve hot, garnished with fresh parsley.

Curried Carrot and Coconut Soup

Ingredients:

- 1 tablespoon coconut oil
- 1 onion, chopped
- 2 garlic cloves, minced
- 1 tablespoon ground curry powder
- 4 carrots, peeled and chopped
- 1 can (14 oz) coconut milk
- 4 cups vegetable broth
- Salt and pepper to taste
- Fresh cilantro for garnish

Instructions:

1. Heat coconut oil in a large pot over medium heat. Add the onion and garlic, and sauté for 5 minutes until softened.
2. Stir in the curry powder and cook for 1 minute until fragrant.
3. Add the chopped carrots, coconut milk, and vegetable broth. Bring to a boil, then reduce the heat and simmer for 20 minutes, until the carrots are tender.
4. Blend the soup until smooth using an immersion blender or a regular blender.
5. Garnish with fresh cilantro and serve hot.

Classic Minestrone with Pesto

Ingredients:

- 2 tablespoons olive oil
- 1 onion, chopped
- 2 garlic cloves, minced
- 2 carrots, peeled and chopped
- 2 celery stalks, chopped
- 1 zucchini, chopped
- 1 can (15 oz) diced tomatoes
- 1 cup green beans, chopped
- 4 cups vegetable broth
- 1 cup small pasta (like ditalini)
- Salt and pepper to taste
- Fresh pesto (store-bought or homemade) for garnish

Instructions:

1. Heat olive oil in a large pot over medium heat. Add the onion and garlic, and sauté for 5 minutes until softened.
2. Add the carrots, celery, zucchini, green beans, and diced tomatoes. Stir for 2 minutes.
3. Pour in the vegetable broth and bring to a boil. Add the pasta and simmer for 10 minutes, until the pasta is cooked al dente.
4. Season with salt and pepper to taste.
5. Serve with a dollop of fresh pesto on top.

Cold Avocado Soup with Lime

Ingredients:

- 2 ripe avocados, peeled and pitted
- 2 cups vegetable broth
- 1/2 cup plain yogurt or sour cream
- 1 tablespoon fresh lime juice
- Salt and pepper to taste
- Fresh cilantro for garnish

Instructions:

1. Combine the avocados, vegetable broth, yogurt, lime juice, salt, and pepper in a blender.
2. Blend until smooth, adding more broth if needed to reach your desired consistency.
3. Chill the soup in the fridge for at least 1 hour before serving.
4. Garnish with fresh cilantro and serve cold.

Curried Squash Soup

Ingredients:

- 1 tablespoon olive oil
- 1 onion, chopped
- 2 garlic cloves, minced
- 1 teaspoon ground curry powder
- 2 pounds butternut squash, peeled and cubed
- 4 cups vegetable broth
- Salt and pepper to taste
- Fresh cream for garnish (optional)

Instructions:

1. Heat olive oil in a large pot over medium heat. Add the onion and garlic, and sauté for 5 minutes until softened.
2. Stir in the curry powder and cook for 1 minute until fragrant.
3. Add the butternut squash and vegetable broth, and bring to a boil. Reduce the heat and simmer for 25 minutes, until the squash is tender.
4. Blend the soup until smooth using an immersion blender or a regular blender.
5. Garnish with fresh cream (optional) and serve hot.

Chicken and Dumplings Soup

Ingredients:

- 2 tablespoons butter
- 1 onion, chopped
- 2 garlic cloves, minced
- 2 carrots, peeled and chopped
- 2 celery stalks, chopped
- 1 teaspoon dried thyme
- 4 cups chicken broth
- 1 1/2 cups cooked chicken, shredded
- 1 1/2 cups self-rising flour
- 3/4 cup milk
- 1 teaspoon baking powder
- Salt and pepper to taste
- Fresh parsley for garnish

Instructions:

1. Heat butter in a large pot over medium heat. Add the onion, garlic, carrots, and celery, and sauté for 5 minutes until softened.
2. Stir in the thyme, chicken broth, and shredded chicken. Bring to a simmer and cook for 10 minutes.
3. In a bowl, mix the flour, milk, and baking powder to form a thick batter.
4. Drop spoonfuls of the batter into the soup. Cover the pot and cook for 15-20 minutes, until the dumplings are cooked through.
5. Season with salt and pepper, and garnish with fresh parsley before serving.

Spinach and White Bean Soup

Ingredients:

- 1 tablespoon olive oil
- 1 onion, chopped
- 2 garlic cloves, minced
- 1 carrot, peeled and chopped
- 1 celery stalk, chopped
- 4 cups vegetable broth
- 1 can (15 oz) white beans, drained and rinsed
- 4 cups fresh spinach, chopped
- 1/2 teaspoon dried thyme
- Salt and pepper to taste
- Fresh lemon juice for garnish (optional)

Instructions:

1. Heat olive oil in a large pot over medium heat. Add the onion and garlic, and sauté for 5 minutes until softened.
2. Add the carrot and celery, and cook for an additional 5 minutes.
3. Pour in the vegetable broth and bring the soup to a simmer. Cook for 10 minutes until the vegetables are tender.
4. Add the white beans, spinach, and thyme, and cook for another 5 minutes until the spinach wilts.
5. Season with salt and pepper, and serve with a drizzle of fresh lemon juice if desired.

Sweet Potato and Black Bean Soup

Ingredients:

- 1 tablespoon olive oil
- 1 onion, chopped
- 2 garlic cloves, minced
- 2 medium sweet potatoes, peeled and cubed
- 1 can (15 oz) black beans, drained and rinsed
- 4 cups vegetable broth
- 1 teaspoon ground cumin
- 1/2 teaspoon smoked paprika
- 1/4 teaspoon chili powder
- Salt and pepper to taste
- Fresh cilantro for garnish (optional)

Instructions:

1. Heat olive oil in a large pot over medium heat. Add the onion and garlic, and sauté for 5 minutes until softened.
2. Add the sweet potatoes, black beans, vegetable broth, cumin, paprika, and chili powder. Stir to combine.
3. Bring to a boil, then reduce the heat and simmer for 20 minutes, until the sweet potatoes are tender.
4. Use an immersion blender to blend the soup until smooth, or leave it chunky if you prefer.
5. Season with salt and pepper, and garnish with fresh cilantro before serving.

Hot and Sour Soup

Ingredients:

- 4 cups chicken or vegetable broth
- 1 cup mushrooms, sliced
- 1/2 cup bamboo shoots, sliced
- 1/2 cup tofu, cubed
- 2 tablespoons soy sauce
- 2 tablespoons rice vinegar
- 1 tablespoon sugar
- 1/2 teaspoon white pepper
- 1 tablespoon cornstarch mixed with 2 tablespoons water
- 1 egg, beaten
- 2 green onions, chopped
- Fresh cilantro for garnish (optional)

Instructions:

1. Bring the broth to a simmer in a large pot. Add the mushrooms, bamboo shoots, and tofu, and cook for 5 minutes.
2. Stir in the soy sauce, rice vinegar, sugar, and white pepper. Bring to a simmer.
3. Mix the cornstarch with water and stir it into the soup to thicken.
4. Slowly pour the beaten egg into the soup while stirring gently to create egg ribbons.
5. Garnish with green onions and fresh cilantro before serving.

Smoked Chicken and Corn Chowder

Ingredients:

- 2 tablespoons butter
- 1 onion, chopped
- 2 garlic cloves, minced
- 2 smoked chicken breasts, shredded
- 3 cups corn kernels (fresh or frozen)
- 4 cups chicken broth
- 2 medium potatoes, peeled and diced
- 1/2 cup heavy cream
- 1 teaspoon thyme
- Salt and pepper to taste
- Fresh parsley for garnish

Instructions:

1. Heat butter in a large pot over medium heat. Add the onion and garlic, and sauté for 5 minutes until softened.
2. Add the smoked chicken, corn, chicken broth, and potatoes. Bring to a boil, then reduce the heat and simmer for 15 minutes until the potatoes are tender.
3. Stir in the heavy cream, thyme, salt, and pepper, and cook for an additional 5 minutes.
4. Garnish with fresh parsley before serving.

Roasted Red Pepper Soup

Ingredients:

- 4 red bell peppers, halved and seeded
- 1 tablespoon olive oil
- 1 onion, chopped
- 2 garlic cloves, minced
- 4 cups vegetable broth
- 1 teaspoon smoked paprika
- 1/2 teaspoon ground cumin
- Salt and pepper to taste
- Fresh basil for garnish (optional)

Instructions:

1. Preheat the oven to 400°F (200°C). Place the red peppers on a baking sheet, cut side down, and roast for 25-30 minutes until the skin is charred.
2. Remove the peppers from the oven and let them cool. Once cool, peel off the skins and set aside.
3. Heat olive oil in a large pot over medium heat. Add the onion and garlic, and sauté for 5 minutes until softened.
4. Add the roasted peppers, vegetable broth, paprika, cumin, salt, and pepper to the pot. Bring to a simmer and cook for 10 minutes.
5. Use an immersion blender to blend the soup until smooth. Adjust seasoning if needed.
6. Serve with fresh basil if desired.

Creamy Tomato and Roasted Pepper Soup

Ingredients:

- 4 tomatoes, quartered
- 2 red bell peppers, halved and seeded
- 1 tablespoon olive oil
- 1 onion, chopped
- 2 garlic cloves, minced
- 4 cups vegetable broth
- 1 teaspoon dried oregano
- 1/2 teaspoon red pepper flakes
- 1/2 cup heavy cream
- Salt and pepper to taste

Instructions:

1. Preheat the oven to 400°F (200°C). Place the tomatoes and red peppers on a baking sheet and drizzle with olive oil. Roast for 20-25 minutes until softened.
2. Remove from the oven and allow to cool. Peel the skins off the peppers.
3. In a large pot, heat olive oil over medium heat. Add the onion and garlic, and sauté for 5 minutes.
4. Add the roasted tomatoes, peppers, vegetable broth, oregano, and red pepper flakes. Bring to a simmer and cook for 10 minutes.
5. Use an immersion blender to blend the soup until smooth. Stir in the heavy cream and season with salt and pepper.
6. Serve warm.

Mushroom and Barley Soup

Ingredients:

- 2 tablespoons olive oil
- 1 onion, chopped
- 2 garlic cloves, minced
- 2 cups mushrooms, sliced
- 1/2 cup pearl barley
- 4 cups vegetable or chicken broth
- 1 teaspoon thyme
- Salt and pepper to taste
- Fresh parsley for garnish

Instructions:

1. Heat olive oil in a large pot over medium heat. Add the onion and garlic, and sauté for 5 minutes.
2. Add the mushrooms and cook for 5-7 minutes until softened.
3. Stir in the barley, broth, and thyme. Bring to a boil, then reduce heat and simmer for 30 minutes until the barley is tender.
4. Season with salt and pepper to taste.
5. Serve garnished with fresh parsley.

Chilled Watermelon Soup

Ingredients:

- 4 cups watermelon, cubed and seeds removed
- 1 cucumber, peeled and chopped
- 1/2 cup fresh mint leaves
- 1 tablespoon lime juice
- 1 tablespoon honey (optional)
- Salt to taste

Instructions:

1. Place the watermelon, cucumber, mint leaves, lime juice, and honey (if using) into a blender.
2. Blend until smooth and creamy.
3. Season with a pinch of salt to balance the sweetness.
4. Chill the soup in the refrigerator for at least 1 hour before serving.

Gingered Pear and Butternut Soup

Ingredients:

- 1 tablespoon olive oil
- 1 onion, chopped
- 2 pears, peeled and chopped
- 1 small butternut squash, peeled and cubed
- 2 tablespoons fresh ginger, grated
- 4 cups vegetable broth
- 1/2 teaspoon ground cinnamon
- Salt and pepper to taste
- Fresh parsley for garnish

Instructions:

1. Heat olive oil in a large pot over medium heat. Add the onion and sauté for 5 minutes until softened.
2. Add the pears, butternut squash, ginger, cinnamon, and vegetable broth. Bring to a boil, then reduce the heat and simmer for 25 minutes until the squash is tender.
3. Use an immersion blender to blend the soup until smooth.
4. Season with salt and pepper.
5. Garnish with fresh parsley before serving.

Baked Potato Soup

Ingredients:

- 4 large russet potatoes, baked and mashed
- 1 tablespoon butter
- 1 onion, chopped
- 2 garlic cloves, minced
- 4 cups chicken or vegetable broth
- 1/2 cup sour cream
- 1/2 cup shredded cheddar cheese
- 1/4 cup chopped green onions
- Salt and pepper to taste

Instructions:

1. Bake the potatoes in the oven at 400°F (200°C) for 1 hour or until soft. Once baked, mash the potatoes and set aside.
2. In a large pot, melt butter over medium heat. Add the onion and garlic, and sauté for 5 minutes.
3. Add the mashed potatoes, broth, sour cream, cheddar cheese, and green onions. Stir to combine.
4. Bring to a simmer and cook for 10 minutes until heated through.
5. Season with salt and pepper to taste.
6. Serve with extra cheddar cheese and green onions on top.

Hearty Kale and Sausage Soup

Ingredients:

- 1 tablespoon olive oil
- 1 pound sausage (Italian sausage works well)
- 1 onion, chopped
- 2 garlic cloves, minced
- 4 cups vegetable or chicken broth
- 2 cups kale, chopped
- 2 medium potatoes, peeled and diced
- 1 teaspoon dried thyme
- Salt and pepper to taste

Instructions:

1. Heat olive oil in a large pot over medium heat. Add the sausage and cook, breaking it up with a spoon until browned.
2. Add the onion and garlic, and sauté for 5 minutes until softened.
3. Pour in the broth, kale, potatoes, and thyme. Bring to a boil, then reduce the heat and simmer for 20 minutes until the potatoes are tender.
4. Season with salt and pepper to taste.
5. Serve hot and enjoy!

www.ingramcontent.com/pod-product-compliance
Lightning Source LLC
LaVergne TN
LVHW081504060526
838201LV00056BA/2920